Fitness

Written by Helen Depree
Illustrated by Bob Kerr

"I am doing push-ups to get fit," said Sharma.

"I am playing soccer
to get fit," said Jake.

"I am skipping rope
to get fit," said Mom.

"I am jogging
to get fit," said Dad.

"I am riding my bike
to get fit," said Grandma.

"I am swimming
to get fit," said Patch.

"We are all fit,"
said the family.